GW00457495

Always

A

Parkstone Girl

Mary Louisa Fisher

Edited, designed and prepared for publication by Suzannah Trickett and Lynda Mole.

Photographs (except where indicated) and content by Mary Louisa Fisher.

No part of this publication may be reproduced, stored in a retrieval system or transmitted in any form or by any means, electronic, mechanical, photocopying, recording or otherwise, without the prior permission of the copyright holder.

Front cover:
Photograph – St Peters Church – Church Road, Parkstone.

Back cover:
Photograph – The Regal Cinema – Ashley Road. Provided by L.Mole.

All enquiries to; Suzannah Trickett – artisanfoodie@yahoo.co.uk

Copyright © 2021 Mary Louisa Fisher

All rights reserved.

ISBN-13: 979 – 8754329720

Acknowledgements

The author wishes to thank her daughter's Suzannah and Lynda, for all their help in putting this book together. I am extremely grateful for all of your efforts in delivering my memories so expeditiously.

Conversion - 12d = 1 shilling 1/- = 5p

Contents

Preface

Due to the success and popularity of my first book "Memoirs of a Child in Poole" published in 2018. I had been asked on numerous occasions for an epilogue.

After hearing some negative talk about Parkstone recently. I decided to write this book of short stories to cheer a little and as a remembrance of the good times, the great area and not forgetting – the good people of Parkstone.

It is an insight into what life was like for me as a child growing up in Parkstone, during the post Second World War period, 1950 – 1960.

The Changes

At one time here in Parkstone, many centuries ago. There was not any education for children if you were poor. The first education was by attending Sunday school.

Their only skills were inherited from Grandparents, or taught by Father and/or Mother at home.

Some usually had a job of work to go to by eight or nine years old. Boys and girls.

Also, the age that you would be able to get married was much less than that it is today. The Age of Marriage Act 1929 under canon law and common law, meant you could marry with parental or guardian consent, at the legal age of puberty. Which was 14 for boys and 12 for girls. However, The Marriage Act 1949 changed the age limit to 16 for both boys and girls with parental or judicial consent or 18 without consent.

These Changes

Every century has had its own story to tell about its children. I have always lived in close proximity to a school for children, both in Poole and Upper Parkstone for many years.

Moreover, during the last century, I have been a witness to many of these changes, the good and the bad that have occurred in the children of today.

This is our New Generation let us hope they have a bright future.

Heritage

My Parkstone Heritage

Came from my Great, Great Grandmother Mary Rowsell, born in Parkstone in 1831. She married Joseph Bartlett in St Peter's Church, Lower Parkstone in 1849. Joseph was born in Canford Magna in 1823 who later became a Master Mariner in Poole.

They had two children both of which were born in Parkstone, a boy and a girl.

Their Son, James Bartlett born in 1851. Their daughter, my Great Grandmother, Agnes Bartlett born in 1853. They also had a further 3 children born in Poole during their marriage. William 1857, Julia 1859 and Jesse 1864.

Mary Rowsell's Father James Rowsell was born in Newfoundland, Labrador, Canada in 1775 during the fishing trade between Poole and Canada. Mary's Grandfather, also named James Rowsell was born in West Monkton, Somerset.

St Peter's Church

My Poole Heritage

Came from my Grandfather Harry John Fisher born in Poole, 1866.

He married a Poole girl, Julia Ansell Bartlett, at St Paul's Church, High Street, Poole. Julia was born in Lagland Street Poole in 1872 and was the daughter of Agnes Bartlett, my Great Grandmother.

Harry and Julia had eight children together. All born in Poole. Four boys and four girls. One of which was my Father, Harold Frederic Fisher. He went on to marry my mother Ethel Maud Bridle in 1933 and then became a "Parkstone Man".

The Fisher's go back many generations of Master Mariners.

My father, Harold Frederic Fisher.

After having received an award for his long time in service at the Cordite factory – 1960.

The Families

There was a great shortage of housing after the Second World War 1939 - 1945 in Poole.

Due mainly to the slum clearance program. Poole had some of the worst slums in England. To name but a few; Gray's Yard and Taylor's Buildings, near to the Quayside. But there were others.

Poole was overpopulated with very small houses containing ten, twelve or even fourteen occupants.

Some moved out to the area of Longfleet. Others immigrated to Canada. Some immigrated to Australia on a cheap ticket dubbed the "Ten Pound Poms". Beginning in 1947 it was one of the largest planned mass migrations of the 20th century. Australia desperately wanted white Brits – under the "White Australia Policy" to increase its population and boost the country's booming industries such as farming. Between 1947 and 1972 more than 1.5 million people moved from Britain to Australia as part of the assisted migration scheme. An opportunity no doubt to escape the post-war rationing and housing shortage. Some 400,000 brits made the trip in the first year alone. My father's Uncle went to Canada. So I must have some distant Fisher relatives there.

But many large families remained living in these terrible conditions. Some did not have running water in their houses. If you needed water, you had to go and collect it from a tap, a shared water supply in the street, using a pail. These were young people starting their married life together.

We can only imagine the suffering.

After the War

My parents would never talk about this time, neither would my two eldest Sister's. It was too much of a painful experience for either of them.

My Father lost a Brother, who of which was only 19 years old in the Great War 1914-1918 in Belgium. The same for my mother also. As she had lost her Brother in France. He was only 21 years old at the time. Ironically, both were named Ernest. Ernest Fisher and Ernest Bridle. Other members of both families died at very young ages through varying illnesses. One of them was my Aunty Millie Crooks (née Fisher) who died from the 1918 Flu Pandemic at the age of 25. Sadly, Aunty Millie had a child, (Vernon Crooks my 1st Cousin), who was only 6 months old at that time. Vernon went on to be raised by his grandparents. My father was only a young man of 14 when the 1st War began, and my Mother was only a child of 6 years old. So not a good start in life for either of them.

I know about this because my parents started their married life in these terrible conditions, along with having two daughters, both of which were born in Poole. Then when struggling to cope with their young family, they were plunged into the Second War 1939-1945. Due to the overcrowding and the diseases of that era, something had to be done about this situation.

So when the building of the Estates began, it must have seemed like "manna from heaven" for the poor people of Poole. Most people were in this state through no fault of their own. Having gone through "The Wars", employment was scarce or poorly paid. No benefits then – of any kind! If you did not work, you had no money simple! They were very proud people, so would not beg. My father worked all his life in the same job, until the day he retired.

The family Allowance started in 1945 which encouraged parents to have more children. To make up for the losses during "The Wars".

Family allowances were the subject of a White Paper in 1942, but there was disagreement among Labour and Conservative politicians about the way they should be implemented.

The Beveridge Report, written by the civil servant William Beveridge, proposed an allowance of eight shillings per week for all children, which graduated according to age. It was to be non-contributory and funded by general taxation. After some debate, the Family Allowances Bill was enacted in June 1945. The act provided for a flat rate payment funded directly from taxation. The recommended eight shillings a week was reduced to five shillings and family allowance became a subsidy, rather than a subsistence payment as Beveridge had envisaged.

Family allowances were introduced in 1946, with the first payments being made on 6 August. At that time, they were only paid for the second child onwards, a further watering down of Beveridge's scheme. In 1952, the Conservative government reduced food subsidies, which had been in place since the war. From October 1952, family allowance was increased by three shillings per week to advance the potential effect on nutrition. As a means of encouraging families to keep children in education, the Family Allowances Act of 1956 extended the family allowance to all school children, although the bread subsidy was abolished. In 1961, Cabinet agreed that the majority of apprentices be excluded from the family allowance provisions, but dismissed proposals that family allowance for the second child be abolished. Family allowance provisions, therefore, remained intact in the Family Allowances and National Insurance Act of 1962.

You had no chance of getting your foot on the property ladder then. Your name was added to the Local Authority Council Housing List, which was very long as you can imagine. So you had a long wait. Simply, it was not a matter of moving up the list as one came off the list. It was deduced by way of a points system to which each couple were given. Priority was given to those in essential services, such as doctors, nurses, midwives and firemen. Even policemen too, if the police force had insufficient housing stock of its own. Then came the families of the greatest of need. Some authorities insisted to get a step towards the top of the list, a couple had to have two children. An incentive that further increases the rapidly rising birth rate. However, in some parts of the country, it was not always guaranteed that you could get a home of your own, as you may have had to share it.

Given the Keys

The first council estate to be built in Parkstone was Trinidad Estate. Nothing to do with the country of that name. More estate's soon followed. The likes of Bourne Estate, Waterloo Estate, Alderney Estate and of course Wallisdown Estate, to name but a few. Of course, these are listed in sequential order.

When a family received "The Letter" from Poole Council, advising them that they have been awarded a house. Contained within the letter was the location and in addition, the words "You do not have to accept it". Of course, your preference for another estate was very short-lived. You soon came to realise that if you were to reject their offer in favour of another location. You would need to be put back on the long and timely waiting list. Some hope!

I can recall my eldest married sister wanting to live on "The Waterloo Estate". When she received "The letter" it was for another location. So, she rejected it! My sister then waited another year until receiving another letter. At last! Her desired location. Hooray!

I cannot begin to imagine the feeling of euphoria. After having lived in squalor and being surrounded by dirt and disease. To, at last, have a brand new house, with gas, electricity, and water on tap... Along with many more rooms. Seemingly, things were on the "UP" in Upper Parkstone.

On the Up

There is great improvement everywhere if you look around on Ashley Road. A variety of new shops, whilst others are being refurbished for a change of business. With many more places now to have tea or coffee with friends or family members. Or perhaps a bite to eat? An array to suit all pallets.

I think the town is now on the up. Forgive the pun! As my mother used to say to me. I am just going "UP on Hill" to do some shopping.

I believe it may take a little while but will once again serve the community.

I miss the "Regal Cinema". In my younger days, I had many a date with a boyfriend from school there. It stood where Iceland is now. Again, some of the old shops, like Woolworths, I see a Polish Supermarket has replaced it. I loved the Co-op that was on the corner of Churchill Road, they sold everything, not only food. There are a great many that have gone, far too many to mention.

But who knows what the plans are for our town's future. Hopeful!

Sorry about the road. But then "it is" the gateway to heaven. Bournemouth, Christchurch and Poole are now known as BCP. I notice that they have left Poole last in their newly formed abbreviation of the area. But not for long eyh as Poole is on the "Up" also.

Parkstone

It was a beautiful autumn morning so I decided to take a walk. There are many places still in Parkstone where you can do this. Quite local, and not too distant from where I am now living, close to the town.

One which I love to frequent is Turners. Opposite the cemetery in Upper Road. In the spring and summer times, it is quite a picture with all the flowering trees.

But right now it is stunning in all its autumn glory.

Also, there is Alexandra Park. Very shady if you cannot take too much sun, and quiet and restful.

Then there is Sea View, at Constitution Hill. Not too far away. But you can always take the number 18 bus from Ashley Road, Upper Parkstone.

What amazing scenery. Enjoy a nice cup of tea or coffee from the mobile van that is parked there. Of which reminds me. Just at the entrance to the view, by the side of the path, was a stone drinking water fountain. You had to put your mouth under the tap and press. The water went all over your face, your hair got wet, and so did your feet. But we were refreshed. We "kids" soon got the hang of it.

Down at Ashley Cross, Lower Parkstone, there is a lovely little park right in the centre of the shops. Somewhere to sit for a lunchtime break, or chat with friends. The trees are a beautiful colour now until the leaves fall.

There is also a beautiful working fountain with cascading water, a sight to behold. The M1 bus from Upper Parkstone will drop you off there if you do not drive a car.

The Fountain

But, if like me, you are an avid walker, Turbary Common is the place to be. "What memories for me". Now it is a Site of Specific Scientific Interest. Scrub, wooded areas, and a "wet and dry" heath. So many important wildlife species, including the Dartford Warbler. And not let's forget, all six species of British reptiles can be found here. There is also a wonderful play area for the children. Another nice place is the Recreation ground, in Recreation Road, if you like open spaces. And all this, only a stones throws away for us all to enjoy.

Welcome to Turbary Common

The Pathways on Turbary Common

The Lakes on Turbary Common

Examples of Plant Life on Turbary Common

The Brook's on Turbary Common

Poplar Tree on Turbary Common

And this is My Story

My Schooldays

In 1947, I was now attending Heatherlands Junior School, located in Cromwell Road, Parkstone. Mr Swan was the headmaster.

Heatherlands Council School, where the "juniors" attended. Was built between two roads, Cromwell Road and Beaconsfield Road in 1891 - 1893. 1898 the infant's department was built. So the school was quite old when I attended in 1947.

We had a bad winter and I can remember it being bitterly cold.

I am referring to the harsh European winter 1946-1947. This caused severe hardships throughout the country. Beginning in December 1946 far-reaching until March 1947. Severe snowfall, reaching 23 feet deep in the Scottish Highlands. Temperatures seemingly plummeting to -21°c in some areas of the country. Major road closures. Some 300 roads were made unusable and railways to being badly affected. Energy, by way of coal and power, was dramatically disturbed, resulting in a lack of supplies. Some coal stockpiles were frozen solid and couldn't be moved, leaving people hurtling out to buy electric fires for their only method of heat. Animals froze to death and farmers lost a staggering amount of livestock. Vegetables couldn't be harvested, resulting in the use of pneumatic drills being used to excavate them. Bringing about rationing for potatoes for the first time in history. Businesses were forced to close, thus putting 4 million people on unemployment benefits. And then came the thaw…. When the warmer weather started to return and the snow and ice began to melt. The country was then hit by severe flooding, causing further devastation. Amid the travesty of having to overcome and still recovering from, the effects of the Second World War to boot.

Of course, I would like to point out at this juncture here, that I am not referring to The Big Freeze 1963. Oh no, "The Big Freeze" remains on record as being the coldest winter, since 1740. The coldest for more than 200 years! Commencing on 29th December 1962, blizzards swept across parts of the UK creating snowdrifts reaching a staggering 20ft in height. These were being fuelled by gale force easterly winds reaching 81 miles per hour (119 miles per hour recorded on the Isle of Man) and temperatures plummeting to -22°c in some parts of Scotland. The snowfall blocked roads, railways and stranded villagers through the loss of power and telephone lines. The seas and rivers were even frozen within some parts of and around the UK. Despite a momentarily brief thaw for three days in January, "The Big Freeze" lasted until early March 1963. When the thaw finally came, along with did the flooding. But, nowhere near anything like the flooding following the thaw as seen in 1947.

But despite these extreme weather conditions, we were all still sent outside to play at break times. Even if it was snowing. But we were wrapped up well to keep warm. I had such great fun playing snowballs with all of my friends.

I have fond memories of Christmas time at Heatherlands. Each year we had a party in our classroom. We had a Christmas tree which was decorated by the children and we would each put presents, tied up on the tree, for our friends. These presents were handed out by our teachers at the end of the day, just before the school would break up for the Christmas holidays. Each child would also have to bring some food to contribute towards the parties that were being held in the classrooms. I usually brought a big bowl of red jelly, which I had made at home under Mother's guidance.

The school is now demolished, but the large brown brick high boundary wall in Beaconsfield Road remains. As are the wide steps leading into Albert Road.

Steps leading to Albert Road.

New houses have now been built on this site. The entrance is on Cromwell Road. But I enjoyed my time here and learnt a lot.

Perhaps you were in my class – 1947 – 1951?

The Journey to School

I can never remember a time being taken to school by any one of my parents. My father, having always left the house very early in the mornings to head out to work. He would catch the train from Poole Railway Station to where he worked at the Cordite Factory, in Holton Heath. As for our mother, she always had plenty to do at home, given we were a large family of eight.

As such, I used to walk to school with my two sisters, Margaret then aged nine, and my younger sister Valerie, a sweet five-year-old. Rounding up our friends along the way. Boys and girls, perhaps you were one of them? There was quite a gang of us by the time we arrived at school. In turn, then on the way home. The crowd gradually dispersed when they reached their homes along the way. Yet, of course, we'd look after each other along (both ways of) the journey.

Often I now watch the neighbours hustling their children into their cars of a morning. Hollering "you're going to be late" or "come along and hurry up". Still, it was very different times back then. Safety wasn't the major cause for concern. You could walk around carelessly at such young ages and felt safe in doing so. Moreover, today most families have one or more cars. Resulting in much more traffic on the roads today! My father never drove. I don't think he ever took a driving test! Hence, never owned a car... Same for mum too. I guess we become a product of our environments, as I never learnt to drive either. Most people could not afford a car, post-war. That was left to the wealthy families. So no chance of my being "Driven to School".

Most of the old houses, built in Upper Parkstone, and Poole, during 1700 - 1800 and 1900 are very noticeable, by the lack of a driveway or garage. Today, parking in the road or at the front of your own house is becoming a problem for homeowners at certain times of the day. Of the houses which have the land and the money to do so, have added an extension of a garage, with a driveway. Other houses with cars are parked up on the patio adjoining the front of their house.

I was recently told you are not now allowed to build a house in Parkstone, without the provisioning of a parking space.

Discipline

School discipline has dramatically changed today. Some I talk to say this is a change for the good, but others tend to feel that the discipline which was enacted, had quite a bearing on the way that the young behave in society today. It produced a greater fear of authority than what exists today. Resulting in a consensus that good manners were more important in society back then.

During school time you were disciplined if you did wrong. In most cases, you were sent to the headmaster's office, where he would decide on what punishment you should receive. Occasionally, the teachers would hand out the discipline. Depending on the severity and more often than not, the

Headmaster would just give you a talking to. That was frightening enough. Or, he would write to your parents and then no doubt they would discipline you themselves. If canning was the Headmasters deciding form punishment, then you would receive six across the hand. Boys and Girls were treated in the same way. "Ouch", but of course not your writing hand, as you might be given 100+ lines to write also. "I must not......" as they would often begin with.

My sister Margaret, who had worked in a school for many years as a dinner lady, since retired. Had told me there is not any physical discipline in the schools today. And in her opinion, this is not a change for the better. The impression portrayed by her is that the children have gradually become very unruly and disrespectful towards authority over time. I can only but imagine, what changes she has seen spanning her 38 years of service.

School Holidays

Springtime

As a young child growing up in the 1950s. We were fortunate to be surrounded by just miles and miles of open moorland for us children to play on.

Back then, it was a paradise for us kids. Our mothers would pack us up each some sandwiches, usually jam, with a bottle of tap water to drink. Off us, all would go for the whole day with our friends. We use to walk for miles on the heath. Well, it seemed like it did, what with our little legs. And being only about eight to ten years old.

I can remember thinking back then, that given we had been on the go for so many hours, I thought it best now to rest awhile. We would all lay down in the long grass. It was a yellow colour like corn, blowing in the light spring breeze, with the sun shining in the blue sky above. Then listening to the sounds of the birds nesting in the trees. To us it was heavenly.

I cannot see a child of eight being allowed to do this freely today. Moreover, they do not appear to have the zest to go off exploring, making camps, climbing trees or newting to name but a few of our adventures. The glorious "great outdoors". Most children I see today, are cooped up in front of a computer screen. So sad really. We had so much energy and exuberance. We so looked forward to our spring and summer school holidays. Another shining example of changes I have noticed in the childhoods of today.

This particular open moorland I am referring to is now the housing estates. Canford Heath and Alderney Estates. Probably about six thousand houses were built on this land.

The Woods at Canford

Quite often in the spring holidays, we would all go off flower picking. For no specific reason, but, for pleasure and the sheer joy of it.

Being out in the fresh air on a spring day was truly wonderful.

It smelt earthy under the trees, with Mother Nature surrounding us all. What an abundance of wildlife to see and touch. Just blissful!

We collected little bunches of wild primroses for our baskets and an armful of bluebells. They would not be too heavy for us to carry home. I could see a lot of fungi, but we did not touch them through fear they were poisonous.

Now feeling a little hungry. We decided it was time to sit and eat our delicious sandwiches, accompanied by our drink of tap water (no fizzy pop for us. That was a luxury). Then when all fuelled up, off to play again before embarking on the long walk home. Arriving safely, all tired and worn out. Dinner was ready and waiting on the table for us to gobble up. Then bath time and bed, "for tomorrow is going to be another lovely day".

Beautiful Primroses

Playtime

Because the Council Estates had very little traffic coming on to them in the 1950s. The children used to play on the unmade roads. There were electric lamp posts that had been erected, that lit automatically when nighttime approached.

Unlike the gas lamps of Poole, which had to be lit by a lamplighter. A man up a ladder. The roads were quite eerie at night. But that was Poole's character then. Our electric lights were much brighter.

During the daytime, we used to draw a "wicket" on the lampposts, with a piece of white chalk borrowed from the school's chalkboard. Which rubbed off very easily when we finished playing a game of cricket. Boys and girls would all play together.

I had many a grazed knee for falling over on the stony road and a small scar to prove it.

Sometimes we would play a game of rounder's using the lampposts as positioning posts for the "fielders" to catch you out at. We didn't need any money to have fun. Too bad if we did! There wasn't any for us. A far cry like the children of today.

When the odd van or car came along slowly, we would just stand aside and let it pass.

Other games we played on the roads were skipping. The girls would have a long thick skipping rope that went right across the road. Any boy or girl would jump in while it was turning and sing at the same time. ♪ *One a penny, two a penny, three a penny – Jump* ♪ Then change places holding the ends of the rope. Such fun!

Summertime

Camping

If the weather was hot and dry, we would go off to make a camp with all of our friends. I knew a place not too far away. Off Herbert Avenue, at the back of the houses in Evering Avenue. There were a lot of tall thick Rhododendron bushes there, which we used to make our camps in.

We were allowed to bring the "chopper" (Axe) from home with us. We needed it to cut a hollow in the centre of the Rhododendron bush. The branches were too thick to be broken by our little hands, so the chopper was a perfect choice. Then using a broken branch, we swept out the middle of the bush. This would be our meeting place during the 6 weeks Summer Holidays.

The boys would climb the trees nearby, so that they could see who was coming to play, from a neighbouring camp. Hopeful that they would be bringing some food and pop to share. Such innocent fun.

We always remembered to take the choppers home with us. As they would be needed in the wintertime to chop the firewood.

The Rhododendrons

Newting

Today, there are still a lot of the local ponds and streams around this area, which I used to play in when I was a child during 1948-1951.

Even my very own children would do the same thing during 1960-1970. It was lovely paddling in the clear cool water.

Then afterwards sitting on the bank, watching the water bubbling over the stones at the bottom. While our feet were drying out, before putting our socks and sandals back on again.

We then went to catch Newts. We'd take along a jam jar, where the lid had a piece of string tied onto it. You had to lay flat on the muddy ground at the edge of the stream, then dip the jar into the stream to catch the Newts. Of course, we got very muddy, but we had our old clothes on, so this did not matter to us. After all, we were having fun! Always challenging by way of competition, seeing who could catch the most. The Newts would be safe in our jars, immersed in pond water. Of course, we always returned them safely back into the stream. Then we all went home for tea covered in mud. "That pleased our Mothers".

Newting Ponds on Turbary Common

Only the Best

Blackberry Picking

August is blackberry picking time. Our mothers would make jam and tarts with them. On occasion, the berries would be served simply on their own accompanied with homemade custard. Yum, yum!

To prepare the blackberries. The night before our mother would soak the berries in salted cold water. This would enable any insects to rise to the top. The insects would then be scooped off in the morning and rinsed thoroughly with fresh cold tap water. Before cooking a little sugar was added for extra sweetness.

We knew where to go for the best blackberries. Mannings Heath Road and Broom Road. In the 1950s these were just very long dusty tracks and the roads met at the bottom of the hill. No Tower Park then. Just lots and lots of blackberry bushes.

When we arrived at our favourite place. We used a stick to reach the highest branches. We always got scratched to death by the prickles on the branches. The enamel dish was soon full of large luscious juicy blackberries. They looked delicious and they most certainly were. I can remember scoffing plenty on the way home. Mum didn't mind, she'd say "there's always tomorrow to go get some more for me". I can remember chuckling to myself and thinking "great, can't wait to get scratched to death again". I guess that's the price to pay for not being able to resist the temptation. Yum!

Blackberries on Turbary Common

Scrumping

If we got very hungry on our adventures, we went scrumping. I knew of some favourite haunts. One of which was at the back of Alderney Hospital. They had a long garden that was full of fruit trees and bushes. Gooseberries, blackcurrants, redcurrants, plus fresh garden peas and carrots among lots of other fruits and vegetables. Sometimes the nurses were in the garden picking beautiful sweet, large golden delicious apples. They would take pity on us poor little hungry urchins and throw some over to us. Not knowing we had already been in and helped ourselves. Naughty little tykes! Stuffing them down our jumpers like the paupers we were. We'd often see the gardener working there. We soon came to realise that if we waited by the fence, the gardener would give some of the delights to us. But sometimes and on the odd occasion, he'd give us a "clip around the ears" if he caught us helping ourselves. The mischievous little beggars we were.

Walking

Longham Bridge

On many days during the summertime. A group of us would walk to Longham Bridge to catch minoes in the river and to also play in the surrounding fields. It was all flat back then. You could see for miles. We would bring a picnic with us and stay all day before embarking on the very long walk home. Always arrived home worn out, very tired and ready for our beds again. This was one of our favourite places.

A child could not do this today. The river is too deep and fast flowing. Although, when I often nowadays pop on the bus from Poole to Ferndown for a day's shopping, I occasionally see families taking a stroll with their dog(s), or a father and son fishing. But I've never seen unaccompanied children playing there as we used to.

Then came the 5th November

Bonfire Night

Hearing the clacking noise going on outside from the newly lit bonfire. I could not but resist writing about it.

Do you remember when we each had a bonfire in our large gardens on the Estates? We all collected things for it in the forthcoming weeks. It was a chance for everyone to get rid of all their rubbish. No money for skips, back then! Then as the days grew closer, became the making of the guy. With Dad's old trousers and shirt. Which he was very reluctant to give up "ha-ha" Mum would say. We'd grab our readymade guy and an old tin mum allowed us to use, then use the coal cart to carry the guy around the roads in Parkstone. Calling out and shaking the tin "please spare a penny for the guy" this was to pay for the fireworks and sparklers. They were not as expensive back then.

With Dad lighting the fire. Telling us all to stand well back, as the flames were high and glowing in the starry sky, along with a multitude of bright colours off all the fireworks. We each were given a sparkler to hold and wrote our names in the air, taking care not to burn one another. Later came the roasting of the jacket potatoes and chestnuts. Which we children collected when going "chest nutting" in October. The potatoes were dug from our gardens. They were served hot accompanied by warming soup, made from our very own freshly picked garden veg. Warming us up inside and out to fend off the chilly winter evening. Then came pudding! Homemade toffee apples, made by our neighbour Mrs Gearing. She used to charge tuppence for each one. A good night of fun was had by all. The evening's entertainment would leave us kids feeling very tired. I can recall going off to bed still with the lingering stench of bonfire smoke up my nose and in my hair.

Childhood

Childhood is a once in a lifetime experience. You cannot go back physically and retake it. My experiences of my childhood, are so very different to those I witness in the children of today.

Togetherness is very important. The memories made will never leave them, or you. It is a great time in their lives to be building a bond that will never diminish, no matter how old they get.

They will learn more from doing things with you, than any book at school or from any computer game sat at home, can teach them. And believe me when I say. That in the years to come, they will not remember that game, neither will they remember the film on the television or tablet/IPad. But they will never forget those momentous times spent together.

My grandson Jaxson.
Enjoying open air pursuits

The Tradesmen

Of all the vans and lorry's which drove around the Estates, to name but a few were;

The Milk Floats

The first deliveries to call in the early hours of the mornings was the milk floats. These were from M & P Dairies which was on the corner of Ringwood and Manning's Heath Road. You would hear the glass bottles of milk rattling in the crates at dawn, as they made their way down the road. It woke everyone up. The milkman would place your full bottles of milk that you had ordered daily on the doorstep. "clink, clink" you would hear as he placed them gently down. Then collecting the "empties" left out by Mum the night beforehand. These were to be taken back to the factory to be sterilised and used again. Every Saturday was a tap on the door "Morning Mrs Fisher, here is your bill" and then Mum would proceed in paying him for the week's deliveries.

Which reminds me. I remember in the very bad winter of 1947, as mentioned previously. The bottles of milk had frozen on the doorstep. The cream at the top had risen two inches above the bottle and the silver cap was protruding off. The milkman still came though despite the bitter weather. Given as the roads were cleared of snow, enabling him to get through. Not easy when it was above your knees. But then, everyone cleared their bit of path at the front of their house.

The Bakers Van

Three times a week the Baker would call to houses on the Estate and ours was one of them.

Lisby's was the name on his van. But they later sold out to Green's Bakery. Many years after, they were known as Kings the Bakers, situated on Wallisdown Road. Another establishment where I worked for many years. But this was much later in my life.

From the open doors at the back of his van, he had a large wicker basket that was filled with lots of fresh bread. All shapes and sizes. From split tin loaves to round Cobbs. Occasionally there were buns too. The smell was divine! He would carry the heavy basket into your house on his arm. All loosely packaged. No plastic wrap like you see today. You then took what was needed and paid him. It was very little money for a loaf back then. Off he went, leaving with a smile and a wave.

The Rag and Bone Man

A lorry used to drive around the roads calling out for "Any Old Iron, Any Old Iron".

My mother sold him her old brass bed. It was no longer needed as they now had another bed made from Walnut. That old bed would have been an antique today and worth a small fortune no doubt. It had been stood outside by the dustbin and only needed a good clean. He gave her very little money for it and then hurtled it up on top of his lorry.

He was also asking for any old woollen things. So I said to mum about a jumper that I had grown out of. Mum went off to look for it in the airing cupboard. "It must be wool", the man said. He gave me a lovely balloon on a stick. I can remember lots of the neighbours giving him things. For a few pence no doubt. I expect he had made a fortune from other people's rubbish.

The Pig Man

There was a special galvanised metal bin with a lid on the top, which was kept outside in the garden. These were known as "Swill Bins".

This was used for any leftover food, "if" there was ever any from mealtimes.

It was not put in the rubbish bins like it is today in Parkstone.

This food waste was for the local Pig Man. He had a big house with a long back garden in Ringwood Road, opposite Trent's Scrapyard. He used to boil it all up together in a big metal bath. This was used to feed his pigs.

He used to collect the bins every week and give you a clean bin. He did not pay you for this. The Pig Man was also a coal merchant. On occasions that I visited the house with our cart to collect coal, you could smell the "Pigs Swill" boiling in the garden.

During the 2001 "Foot and mouth outbreak" it was believed that unprocessed "pigs swill" was a link in the chain of infection and subsequently banned in Great Britain in 2002. However today, in some counties, there are specific "food waste" bins collected every week. Not something I've seen in Parkstone. Why is this? This waste is then processed and when broken down it produces Biogas which is extracted and used to generate electricity. What a fabulous idea! Once the gas has been extracted, the remaining liquid is used as fertiliser on farmland. Win, win!

The Walls Ice Cream Van

It came every day of the week playing its music, then with a final "Ding Dong" before stopping outside someone's house. Usually, it was on a corner. We lived in Trinidad Crescent and our house was situated on the corner. How fortunate was I? On hearing the ringing bells of the ice cream van, feelings of excitement raced through me. On Sunday afternoon's I bought a "block" of Walls Vanilla ice cream for two shillings (10p), and cut it up to share with the family. Wall's ice cream is still my favourite, even today. Brings back so many good memories of times gone by. Memories of when as children we were all together.

The Coalman

Every house on the estate had solid fuel fires. Coal, coke or log fires. The houses were built with fireplaces in many of the rooms, no central heating then.

The coal lorry used to arrive with lots of bags of coal and delivered to several houses in the road. The Coalman carried the sacks upon his back. He would empty the sacks into a bunker or coal shed, about hundredweight bags. The coal dust used to fly up all over him when he dumped them down. Leaving him with a black face and hands. I can all but imagine how dirty he and his clothes were by the end of his day. "I bet his wife or mother looked forward to welcoming him home".

Pigeon Fanciers

The Pigeons

It was around 1950 that my father took an interest in pigeons and decided to keep a few.

First, a loft had to be built for them. So with the help of my only brother John, who was a young man at that time, they set about making the frame work out of old wood. Then connected slightly thicker sheets of wood to the framework. By leaving an opening at the front so that the birds could enter, but not exit. It was quite a big job, but between the two of them, they managed it.

We had a very long back garden, which was full of growing fruit and vegetables, with a gravel path leading down through the middle. It ran the whole length of the plot. They placed the loft at the very far end against our wire boundary fence. The roof had to be felted and made waterproof. A door was added, with a padlock fitted. Then the whole loft was painted with a wood preserver.

Join the Club

It became a great hobby of his. Something Father and his only Son could enjoy together. They both became members of a pigeon club, where they made lots of friends. Male and also female, with the same interests, birds "Of the feathery kind, of course".

Breeding

Dad began by fitting out his loft with lots of nesting boxes. He kept his birds clean by scraping inside of the loft often. He did not mind the mess. After all, pigeon poop was very good for the garden. He loved his birds and was very gentle with them. After a time, he became a breeding expert and only had the best. It was a joy for him and gave him great pleasure.

Racing

He had about sixty birds, which took a lot of feeding. So they decided to join a racing club. They would enter their very best pigeons into competitions in the hope of a win. Not only for the pleasure and thrill of it but to make some money to help with the expense.

Champions

My brother now had a loft of his own. This he had bought and was situated on the other side of our garden.

Dad and my brother John did have some great birds which won many trophies and prizes. They were champions! My father Harold taught his son all that he had learned. This "togetherness" they shared all of their lives.

The only downside for us children was that on race days we were not allowed to play in the garden. But I used to love watching the birds from my bedroom window at the back of our house. They would fly around the house and land on the loft roof. It was quite spectacular to watch and enjoy.

Moving Up

Back to School

Now September 1951 and following my recent 11th birthday in August, I shall be attending a new school for girls. A fledging senior nonetheless. Kemp Welch Secondary Modern. It was segregated from the boy's school. My favourite subjects were history, geography, and cookery, now known as domestic science.

School discipline was still being enacted at this school. I remember a time when getting my knuckles cracked with a ruler by a teacher, for talking to a girl in class, and not paying attention. But I soon learnt not to do this and went on to enjoy my time there.

The Parkstone Girls

I still remember;

Marlene Brake
Katherine Gollop
Sylvia Burt
Valerie Sargeant
Maureen Burden
Gwendoline King
Audrey Sibley
Primrose Baker
Anita Taylor
Fay Reynolds
Vera Gobel
Janice Shearing
Pam Real
Valerie Kitkat
Beryl Ford
Ann and June Ball (twins)

Home Help Needed

Caring

A girl at school approached me during our playtime break. She was not one of my usual friends. She began to tell me about a lady who was an invalid due to an accident and needed some help at her home. She explained that the lady was offering half a crown pocket money to "the right person". The duties required would be after school time, around 4 pm. I said I would have to ask my mother. Mother agreed but said that I must still carry out my usual errands which took place on Saturday's at my grandmother's house. As she was requiring help also.

Unknowing to me at that time. The experience I gained whilst working here, would soon become invaluable to me. This became the start of my career as a Carer, which I undertook later in my life.

Not What I Expected

This lady was an exceptionally talented oil painting artist, a fine Seamstress and a great reader and writer of humorous poetry. This displayed her good sense of humour when reading in a real Dorset Dialect. She did make us all laugh. Her name was Dorothy Beatrice Hills (Née Loveland) but everyone called her Auntie Dorothy, including myself. Although not my real Auntie. A resident of Lincoln Road in Upper Parkstone.

My main job was to help Nan, her "live in" housekeeper/carer and to do all the food shopping. There were quite a few local shops in the area. I was always given a list of goods to buy and the money to pay for them. I suspected Nan was of retirement age.

Making a Living

Dorothy was always a very busy lady. When she wasn't working on a painting. Which I seem to recall, was rather quite a messy job with all the brushes and her tubes of oil paints spread all around her. She would be busy on her bed making rag dolls from scratch, for little children.

I can remember being asked on many occasions, to fetch a large suitcase for her from behind the settee, situated in front of the bay window. This suitcase contained all of the materials needed for her to do the job.

Sometimes I had to buy "offcuts" for her from Labetts. A fabric shop in Ashley Road, Upper Parkstone. I would need to catch the little Rossmore bus for this task.

The dolls' bodies were as soft as silk. I can imagine that any child would love to cuddle them. Their faces and hair she made herself. Some had dark hair, some had blonde. Dorothy would then dress them in the most beautiful satin handmade dresses and bonnets, all pretty colours. When they were finished she would wrap each one in tissue paper. To be sold for five shillings each. Such delicately and detailed high quality, time-consuming work.

Always a Welcome

Auntie Dorothy's house was very 1930s inside. She was a little bit eccentric and did not like change. Nothing modern about her! But she did have some nice old things. The house was made comfortable with lots of pretty cushions, all homemade by her. I do not believe there was ever a day when a visitor or friend did not call in to see how she was keeping. The tea tray was always ready for them. Sometimes a slice of cake is made by Nan. Coffee and walnut was a keen favourite.

The Summerhouse

When the weather was nice, either in the spring, summer, or autumn. Her friends would push Auntie Dorothy outside in a wicker bath chair. Far too heavy for Nan or myself to operate.

In her back garden was a pretty little Summerhouse. Not like today's all glass types, as that would have been too hot for her inside. We would open up the large wide wooden doors. Dorothy loved it out there amongst her flowers and listening to the sound of the birds, singing in the trees all around her. Often she would stay outside in her garden until Sunset.

Aunty Dorothy outside in her garden sitting in the Wicker Bath Chair, with me alongside her, aged 13.

Never a Dull Moment

Dorothy always kept herself busy with her painting. She very much enjoyed reading, always keeping a book to hand, between her many visitors. Everyone in the road where she lived, at number 71 knew of her.

Many school children called in on their way home from school. No child, however dirty or ragged they looked was ever turned away. She could always see their funny side and the good in them. Sometimes she would help them with their reading if they were a little slow at school. Giving them praise and the confidence to succeed and many did.

She was also renowned to help anyone in the area that had a problem. Many would call in on her. She took her time to talk it through with them and try to help. She usually did. They on most occasions left feeling a lot happier.

An Amazing Woman

Although she became bedridden because of trouble with her spine for which she received treatment at home. This did not stop Auntie Dorothy from living her life to the full.

An article appeared in the local paper with a photo of Dorothy Hills surrounded by many children in her garden. Around 20 of them. The heading "A Home for Broken Hearts".

As the saying goes, "the good die young" but not in her case. Dorothy was taken into White Cottage Retirement Home in Parkstone, after having a fall at her home. Dorothy passed away peacefully at White Cottage on 26th

Dorothy Hills
03/03/1899 – 26/10/2002
Source: Joan Hallett (Née Loveland)

October 2002. I had spoken with her earlier in that year, she was 103 and still knew who I was. A remarkable woman.

Parkstone People

Have a character that is like no other. I know of this because of living here in Upper Parkstone for seventy years. Additionally, I consider myself a well-travelled lady. On my travels, I have clearly distinguished a profound difference in other parts of the British Isles.

A true Parkstone person is friendly and always has a smile for everyone. Even if approached by someone they do not know you, they will lend a helping hand if needed.

Or perhaps to stop for a little chat, especially if you have a dog with you. They are real dog lovers here.

It must be something to do with the hills. "Life here in Parkstone is all Up's and Down's".

I have never met a nasty Parkstone person.

It is still a very nice place to live. I am not biased. I was born in Poole after all.

The Flower Sellers

I can still remember the many different characters, which were around Parkstone during 1950-1960.

One of which was the Flower Sellers. With their little bunches of wild heather. Picked off the common. "For Luck Lady" they would say. Or others with a large basket full of the most beautiful flowers.

They used to sit on a stool and sell them to the people passing by. Well, at least you got something nice for your pennies. They also sat upon a stool outside Woolworths in Bournemouth Square. Now Boots the Chemist. I can still picture her now, quite a large lady wearing a black trilby hat.

Not So Different

There were a lot of travellers around in my young days, full of character. The ones I had the pleasure to meet were very nice people. Some attended Kemp Welch School so that they could learn to read and write.

Most lived in houses of their own. They were hard-working people too. I had two friends Janet and Molly Turner, who were sisters. They lived in a bungalow at Rosemary Road.

There was always a welcome for me from their mother Jannie. Their home was very frugal, with no carpets on the floors, but clean and respectful.

When our six-week summer school holiday started, the whole family went hop picking. I was asked to go with them but was not allowed by my parents.

I will never forget their smiles.

The Gypsy's

The Kings were a Gypsy family. Often Gypsy's are very misunderstood. Their house was in Rossmore Road, the Albert Road end. Mrs King wore a long skirt with lots of petticoats beneath it. With a long apron over the top. Her hair was plaited around her head. She was a very proud lady and a very attractive woman.

Facing her house across the road, was a shop where I worked as a young girl. She used to pop into this shop occasionally. When paying for her goods, she would pull up the skirt showing off her petticoats. Because, here is where she carried her purse. In full view of other customers waiting to be served. You can imagine the despair! But of course, they were very clean. I expect she had lived in a real gypsy caravan at one time in her life.

The Stanley's

The Stanley's lived in Lincoln Road at the very bottom of the hill. This was another nice family of travellers and very hardworking people.

I knew the girls at school. They were always nicely dressed with very long pretty hair. You could not help but admire their home and garden when passing "it was a picture". With shades over each window during the summer months and baskets of flowers hanging on each wall of the Bungalow. In the garden were rows of the most pretty colourful flowers planted in a raised bed along the driveway. I often saw a lady attending them, with Pride!

The Coal Merchants

Another true Parkstone family was the Meadens in Rossmore Road. What a nice happy lot they were. Ada, Polly, Frank, Charles, Maggie, Ray and Pauline, but mostly I remember Phil. "The Coal Man".

He always had a smile for you. Which could not have been easy for him with a heavy sack of coal on his back. He would always wave from the lorry if he saw you out and about. He had a house near the shop where I worked. So his wife Penny, did her shopping every week with us at Millers in Rossmore Road. Along with the other members of the family. Always popping in with their children for something or another.

The Kitcher's, three doors down from the shop, was also a very nice family of Merchants. They had a little boy called Terry I believe and a girl called Jenny.

Turner's Nursery

I remember passing this Nursery often on my way "Up on Hill". Often being the term for which was Ashley Road, Upper Parkstone was known. On one side of it was a consolidated dirt path about twenty-foot wide, with trees on either side. It began at the top of Upper Road opposite Brixey Road. This hilly pathway sloped gradually to the bottom end of Uppleby Road. A shortcut for me. As at Eleven years old in 1951, I had already walked the whole length of Brixey Road to reach it from Trinidad Estate. And I still had the long Uppleby Road to tackle.

The path was not lit then. So I must get back to it before dark. Or I would have to walk the long way round, to get to my home. Which I sometimes did.

Walking downhill was fine, but not so much fun going back up. Especially if you had a bag of heavy shopping to carry. Or a "Silver Cross" pram to push. As I soon came to do later in my life.

On the other side of Turners Nursery is Victoria Road and also the gates to Branksome Cemetery in Upper Road. The Land which Branskome Cemetery is built upon, belonged to William Turner's Grandfather, also a Parkstone Man. He left this land specifically to the Poole Council for them to build the Cemetery, for him to be buried there when the time came.

The gate into the Nursery was in Victoria Road.

Many years ago, if you were a child and waited by this gate, someone would open it and hand you some fresh vegetables to take home. Maybe it was Mr Turner senior? There was a stream on the other side of the road. Where the young children could play. But not anymore, as now stands a row of very nice bungalows in its place.

That Path

At one side of the Nursery, this has now been re-surfaced by the Poole Council and street lamps installed. A Pathway for pedestrians and cyclists only. No cars!

That Path - Image 1

That Path - Image 2

The trees have grown huge on each side of the path. There are Oak and Sycamore giving shade when needed to plants beneath their feet. Lots of Bluebells at times.

A very beautiful walkway for everyone to enjoy.

A Parkstone Man

William Turner – Owner of Turners Nursery

Some of his land he gave to the Parkstone People. The Poole Council have now made his land into a Beautiful Park.

For all to enjoy including the dogs. Many new young trees are now in flower and are being protected until established.

All kinds of hedgerows have now grown for nesting birds and what a joy to hear. I also noticed lots of wildflowers for the bees. A buzzing sound fills my ears.

The flowering shrubs are at their best - Bridles wreath was covered in white with a pink shamrock at its feet.

An area has been allocated for fruit trees. Which are now in blossom.

It has an unlocked gate. A notice says "please shut the gate on leaving" and that dogs are allowed, but they must be kept on a lead in the park.

I see a lot of blackberry bushes too, which will be ripe for picking in July or August time. No doubt the blackbirds will devour them.

There are some new seats now in the park. A place for the young or old to sit awhile and chat with friends or with other dog lovers. The grass is kept clean and freshly mowed.

Fenced off next to the park is a Wild Woodland Area. It has been untouched for many years. Wild animals, such as foxes, rabbits, birds and insects live here.

Beautiful Park

Wild Woodland Area

A truly great Parkstone Man! Who has and still is, giving so much pleasure to so many people including myself.

The Grave

While visiting Branksome Cemetery, I noticed his grave. It is located on the left-hand side just inside the lower gates. So not so far away. Still keeping an eye on things for us.

Must take some flowers next time. "As a big thank you".

The Brown House

At the top of the hill in Upper Road, on the left side going up, just before Brixey Road which is on the right. Stands a pair of brown brick semi-detached houses. These houses have always puzzled me when passing them. Why were only those two houses built on all this land? Even after the Second War 1939-1945 when there was such a shortage of housing in Poole and Parkstone.

I thought it must be where the landowner lived with his family? No! I was told. A man named Mr Brock lived in one of them who kept his horses on the grass nearby. Just after the war, during 1945-1950. Any child that wanted a ride on one of his horses, would have to pay him 3D.

Upper Parkstone

I am pleased to see it has still retained a lot of its character, with the beautiful large houses and cottages. Yes! There is still one in Churchill Road. Approximately four hundred years old! But there are others. Also, some very old lovely houses around that have not been lost to time. Buckland Road and Victoria Road, at the top end and also Jubilee Road, has some old properties. All blending in well with the new.

For many a reason, at some points in my life, I have walked down every Road in Upper Parkstone and lived on a few.

And So the Work Begins!

Leaving School

In August during the summer holidays, I had reached my fifteenth birthday. 15 was the school leaving age in 1955. It felt very strange to me that I would not be returning to school at the start of the new term in September. School had always been a very large part of my life.

A Job of Work

I can recall the employment officer coming to Kemp Welch School, to talk with all of the pupils that were leaving that year. They would ask what your interests were and then offer you good advice on how to get started.

Employment

In 1955 when I left school, you did not go looking for work. It came looking for you. Potential employers would contact the schools around the end of term time, looking for staff to hire. There was an abundance of work available.

Advertisements were placed in the local papers. Firms needing young apprentices, builders wanting young trainees and labourers (of all ages). Company's such as; Hamworthy Engineers, through to factory's like; Parrs, a confectionery factory well renowned for Bournemouth and Poole's seaside rock. Pineland Laundry, Wallis Tin, Max Factor, Websters, Millers in Poole, Corona and not forgetting Ryvita. I worked at the Ryvita factory in the 1960s for 8 years. Others were the retail outlets, like; Marks & Spencer's and Woolworth's. The list was endless. The world was our oyster! I did not know anyone that was not employed. "It was called Pride".

My First Real Job

There was a grocery and hardware shop named Millers in Rossmore Road, Upper Parkstone, which I used to frequent. The owners knew me quite well. One day while doing a little shopping at their store, they asked me if I had left school. I said yes, "well how about you coming to work for us then?" they said. "We require a full-time shop assistant"! I replied, "yes please". That is how I got my first real job!

The Weekly Wage

I was told what my hours would be each week, the weekly wage and that I would have to pay a National Insurance Contribution.

My hours were;

Monday, Wednesday, Thursday, Friday and Saturday 8 am until 6 pm, with one hour off for lunch at 1 pm. On Tuesday's it was half-day closing, so I only worked until 1 pm. I did have a coffee break in the mornings at 11 am and a tea break, in the afternoon around 4 pm.

My weekly wage was £4 20d, after NI.

Never on Sundays

The sign on the door read closed. Of course, it should do as it is a Sunday after all. Stores would never open their doors on a Sunday. It was not a law for small corner shops. But considered as a religious day. So that people could attend church if they choose to. Our local churches were; The Good Shepherd in Herbert Avenue, St John's Church at Ashley Road, Upper Parkstone or an establishment of their choosing, dependent upon religion. Sunday's were considered a day of rest. My father would not even allow my mother to do any washing on a Sunday.

Early Closing

The shops in Ashley Road Parkstone, the High Street in Poole and large shopping Centres like Bournemouth. Had early closing on a Wednesday, for as long back as I can remember. But it was nice to go window shopping. As the windows were always dressed very nicely. Also, all the prices were displayed. This was a "nice touch" as you could work out what you would like to buy and then go back when they opened on the next day.

Working Girl

I was awoken by my mother with a nice cup of tea about 06:30. "Mary," she said "time to get up, you do not want to be late on your first day", "Breakfast is on the table downstairs". It was Monday morning. I sipped my tea to wake myself up, then sprung out of my bed and headed for the small bathroom. Fortunately for me, it was vacant. My father and four of my siblings had already used the bathroom and were already having their breakfast before they too all went off to work. In 1955, my mother was the only person left in our household that didn't go out to work. As my father would not allow it. "A women's place is in the home" he would say. As if she did not have enough work to do at home? After all, that was her full-time job. My, how things have changed! Setting aside, my youngest sister who was only eleven years old, left at home, but of course, she was still at school.

My First Day

I arrived a little earlier. As I knew my new employer's needed to have a talk with me and to take me around the premises, before opening the shop. I was shown by the proprietors where to hang my coat etc. It was in a corner of the storeroom. There was a mirror on the wall with a shelf beneath it, ready to use if I needed to refresh my face and hair during the daytime. I was given by Mrs Miler a nice light green overall to protect my clothes. Stating that it would be replaced with a clean one as needed. Then I was shown where the cloakroom (toilet) was situated.

Opening up the Shop

One of my many responsibilities was to open up the shop door in the mornings. I was told where the large keys were kept. On the door, there was a cream blind, which shot up quickly making a whacking sound when I pulled on the cord. On the top was a bell. Anyone opening or closing the door would make it ring. This was a great help if I was putting away stock in the storeroom. I could then hear the bell ring if a customer entered the shop.

On the outside walls at the front of the shop, were two very large roller blinds over the windows. Mr Miller said he would pull them out, as they are too heavy for me to operate. He used a long pole with a hook on the end of it. They kept the sun off the windows and so the shop kept cool in the summertime.

The Shop

Miller's was considered a corner shop, but not on a corner. It was very much like the shop in the television program "Open All Hours", but larger and better. Mr Miller was a very smart gentleman, as he had served in the Navy during the Second World War. Mr Miller whilst working in the shop and serving his customers, wore a brown overall coat. Very much like the one worn by Ronnie Barker in Open All Hours, and the same for David Jason, in the repeat version of the show "Still Open All Hours". Makes you laugh, but it was very true. Mrs Miller was a very nice lady. She had a lot of patience and spoke softly to everyone.

The Clock

As you approached the serving counter, high upon the wall, was a very beautiful brass ships clock. It was the boss's pride and joy. He would always keep it nicely polished. No doubt a reminder of his days in the Navy. He did tell us that his ship was torpedoed during the war and that he was rescued with only his watch. Overlooking the obvious that he failed to mention "His life of course"!

Showing me the Ropes

Mr and Mrs Miller the shop owners, lived right next door. There was an interconnecting door which gave you access directly into the shop from their house. When a customer would enter the shop, you could hear the bell ring from inside the house. This would allow either Mr or Mrs Miller to enter the shop and attend to their customers when they were needed. Which was very handy when I was new to the job and still learning the ropes. Particularly when I was being shown where everything was kept, as you couldn't keep your eye on the counter if you were "out the back" of the shop. Most of the customers were their neighbours or "the locals". Understandably being introduced to them, meant that I met a lot of friendly people. Another job that kept me busy was refilling the shelves against the walls. The stock which I would get from the storeroom. I would first of all have to wipe over the new stock, wipe the shelf and ensure that the labels were facing forward. This meant that the customer was able to find what they needed at first glance.

Nothing Automatic

There were not any automatic tills in this shop, but a cash drawer, set into the countertop. This had a paper roll inside, which you would have had to write the total of goods which had just been sold. I was the only "human" calculating machine here! If there were only just a few items, I could just add them up quickly in my head. I was always very good at maths at school. However, we never used to call it maths, it was known as "mental arithmetic" in my school days. I learnt all of my times tables off by heart. If the customer had a list of goods needed, I would just write the prices on the paper and then total them up speedily. Getting it correct was of the utmost importance, so you could give the right change. Cash only then, no cards, but occasionally a cheque if the customer was well known to us.

Up the Ladder

We not only sold food but hardware too. It was only light household things. But this was very good, as it saved people a journey into town. As it meant that they would need to catch the little Rossmore bus and then have to lug it all the way home again. So this was advantageous to our customers. We stocked buckets and bowls, all shapes and sizes. Brushes, brooms, floor mops and cloths of all kinds. Dustpans with matching hand brushes, along with whistling kettles and teapots. The trouble for me was, it was on the very top shelf all around the shop.

Apart from the brushes and broom handles, as they were kept in the storeroom. I seemed to spend a lot of my time going up and down a ladder. But if it was a large or heavy item the boss would fetch it down for me.

Cleaning Day

As Tuesday is early closing for us and not our busiest morning. I would do any light cleaning that needed to be done in the shop. I'd start early, so by the time the customers would start to arrive I was almost finished.

The counter is about 8ft long, fairly wide, and very heavy as to hold weight. It is wooden and made from Pine with a smooth top. No doubt from all of the wear it has received over time. In the middle of the counter is a beautiful scale with brass weights. This had to be polished until it shone. Regularly, the Weights and Measure people would come round to check the accuracy of the scales. Every Tuesday, I would have to remove everything off of the counter. Mrs Miller would bring a bowl of hot soapy water from her kitchen, along with a soft brush and cloth, for me to clean the countertop.

The Floor

For this job, Mr Miller would hand me a bucket full of sawdust. Which contained Pine Disinfectant it smelt lovely. He said "sprinkle it all over the shop floor, one area at a time" "Then leave it for a while before sweeping it all backup, using the hand shovel and brush, putting the sawdust back into the bucket". This cleans the floor without water and keeps the dust down on the shelves.

The floor was always dirtier where the potato sacks were kept. This was in the far corner of the shop. Potatoes were sold loose with the soil still on them. This is why this area was always dirtier than the rest of the shop. There stood also, was different scales to weigh the potatoes. These were much larger than the scales on the serving counter. These had black heavyweights and a brass bowl. This too had to be cleaned on occasions.

But not now "it's coffee time"!

Coffee Break at Eleven O'clock

This was a twenty-minute break.

Mrs Miller always made the most wonderful ground coffee served by a jug.

She would say to me "fetch a plate of the loose biscuits from the shop". We would have our coffee breaks sat around a table in their sitting room. Clever that door which was leading into the shop, as it meant we would take it in turns to get up and serve a customer when hearing the shop doorbell ring. There were always two new magazines delivered each week. The Woman and

Womans Own. This was particularly handy as these we would read whilst we'd enjoyed our coffee. Mr Miller usually read a little of the daily paper.

Afterwards, I returned to finish my work in the shop until lunchtime at 1 pm. I went home for this usually. Ready and waiting was a salad prepared for me by my mother. Using fresh ingredients from our garden. Yum!

The Deliveries

Tuesday was delivery day. Before the shop would close at 1 pm, the deliveries would begin to arrive. The first was the vegetable lorry. I would see him pull up and then rush over to the door to open it up for him. The driver was heading in carrying a large sack of potatoes. He placed them in the area especially for the potatoes away from other goods. He then returned to the lorry with Mr Miller, who came back in carrying a wooden box filled with local tomatoes. They smelt like they had just been picked from the garden. I placed them titled up, right at the end of the counter next to the bacon and ham cabinet. I would leave them covered until tomorrow morning. Then when the customers arrived the next day, I would remove the cloth to catch the eyes of the customers. They were sold at two shillings a pound, but you could just have one or two if that's all you needed.

The Danish Bacon

A very large van was parked outside the shop on the road. A man was coming towards the store and carrying over his shoulder, was a whole side of smoked bacon. Very heavy for him I should imagine. He was shown where to put it by Mr Miller. Mr Miller would immediately bone some of it, ready for the slicing machine on Wednesday morning. The Bacon was kept in a large cabinet inside the storeroom. The storeroom was leading off from the shop and was much, much cooler in there.

The Egg Man

Next to arrive was the egg van from a local farm. They were not packed in little boxes like today. But in indented cardboard trays, about two dozen in each. The man brought in about 20 trays of eggs, all different sizes. Lovely brown and white. These we stacked on a white tiled shelf.

The Cheese

The Cheese has just arrived. And I mean cheese! Not in the packets like today. But a whole big round of matured Cheddar Cheese coated in a muslin wrap.

At 15 years old I was taught how to skin cheese. You'd have to be very careful because the knife is extremely sharp. Tomorrow I will skin it. The boss would lift it onto a wooden board, as far too heavy for me. Using a wire cutter, he would cut the first wedge out of it. Oh my Goodness! The smell is heavenly. Licking my lips with bated breath. Some he placed on a wooden cheese board with a fixed wire cutter. This was placed upon the cool white-tiled shelf, ready and waiting to serve our customers. But first and foremost; at last, we both have a taste! Yum, fresh cheese! It's gorgeous! Before placing a cover over it. The price you paid for cheese back then was a fraction of today's prices.

The rest of the whole cheese goes back in its place, in the storeroom keeping it cool until needed. No refrigeration! Just a cool storeroom.

Bacon and Ham Day

I enjoyed my half-day off yesterday. So arrived nice and early. As Wednesday is a busy day for us all. Carol a local girl, another shop assistant will be coming in later to help with the serving of customers. Carol always had a smile for everyone.

Learning the Trade

On each end of the counter, stands large glass cabinets. One is for the sliced bacon, pieces of bacon for boiling at home and cooked sliced gammon ham. There are several white trays inside for this purpose. The other glass cabinet was full of chocolate bars.

Today I am being taught how to bone bacon. Collar, Back and Streaky. All in preparation for slicing on the bacon and ham machine. "Very sharp and scary" and there is a knife guard. But fear not! Mrs M, as all called her, will show me how to work it. The Gammon is now in her kitchen being slowly boiled for slicing tomorrow on Thursday.

Skinning the Gammon

Today is Thursday. When I was about to start work in the shop. I noticed hidden from the view of the customers, at the back of the store, was a very large cold cooked Gammon covered in a thin white string netting. At that moment, Mr M entered the shop from their house and he said to me "I would like to show you how to skin the Gammon". Mrs M went into the shop to take over from me to serve the visiting customers.

The ham was placed on a big white board, so as not to make a mess. The first thing I had to do was cut off the string net.

Then I had to remove the thick brown skin with a sharp knife. It came off easily. Leaving the ham covered in a soft white fat. Now comes the best part. To cover it all over with golden breadcrumbs.

Mrs M said to me that she would shortly begin slicing some of the ham on the bacon machine. This would then be placed on the white tray in the glass bacon cabinet ready for sale. It smelt gorgeous and tasted wonderful. To this day I have never known ham so good.

We sold it at two shillings a quarter pound. When serving a customer gammon, we would use the scales situated in the middle of the counter. You would have to lay a sheet of greaseproof paper on the white plate of the scale and using a sliver spatula you would place the freshly sliced gammon on the paper. Once weighed, it was then wrapped into a white paper bag. This was on Thursday's, but by the end of the day on Saturday, the whole Gammon was completely sold out!

The Local Deliveries

The Delivery boy arrived at 4 pm. His name was Leonard Beasley. He was a tall young man with lots of short curly hair. I knew Leonard, as he was in the boy's section of my school and we became friends. Everyone liked him, he had a very lovely smile.

Mr Miller had a bike in the shed at the back of the property ready for him to make deliveries. It had a wide flat metal tray at the front of the handlebars to carry the boxes. It was one of my jobs to get the boxes ready for him when he had to do the local deliveries. He had been doing deliveries for Mr and Mrs M long before I started working here. So knew the customers and their addresses well. The deliveries took about an hour and a half as Len had to make several trips. This was mainly because he could only take one box at a time. Once the deliveries were made, Len would lock the bicycle away for tomorrow, as more deliveries were needing to be made.

Easter Time

The chocolate glass case, at the end of the counter, was full of the most beautiful Easter Eggs. All hand decorated with sugar flowers. There was a notice saying "orders now being taken".

The baker had just arrived with fresh bread for the day and much like at home, it was all unwrapped and unsliced. Also brought with him, was a large wooden tray full of Hot Cross Buns. The smell was gorgeous in the shop.

Dried Salted Cod

On Good Friday, our father made us children eat cooked salted codfish. He said we had to suffer just as Jesus did for us. And suffer I did! But we all cheered up later when we had Hot Cross Buns for tea. But the Cod was soon a distant memory when we received our beautiful Easter egg on Easter Sunday.

A Very Personal Service

It took time to serve each customer, meaning others had to wait their turn. But during this time you got to know them and a lot about their lives.

To give you a little insight. If our finest English Cheddar Cheese was asked for. I had to cut a piece with a wire, place it on a sheet of greaseproof paper and weigh it. Then ask the customer is this okay"? It should never be too much, or too little. Just exactly what the customer wanted. You would then advise them of the cost before packaging nicely. This service took time. Serving a customer in the '50s was completely different to what I experience today. Service was a very personal affair, you spent your time caring about them and most importantly making sure they were happy. Their regular custom was your backbone. You needed them as much as they needed you.

Community Spirit

It was also an opportunity for the people to catch up with their community peers. People spoke to one another whilst waiting to be served by one of us four assistants. Everybody knew everyone. It was truly a joyful experience to watch.

Time for Some Fun

Growing Up

I was enjoying my job at the shop and earning money. So I was now able to pay Mother for my keep at home.

That little brown envelope I received each week, full of cash for my working week. It was a nice feeling. It gave me something that I had never experienced in my life before now "Choice". Also to become a little independent.

It was not a lot of money. But in 1955 things were a lot cheaper than they are today. You learnt how to save your money. You had respect and understood the true value of money. When you desired something, you didn't borrow the money for it. You saved up. Which gave you a sense of achievement. I see the teenagers of today, borrowing all the time, what with student loans etc. But for me, I could now have a social life after work with my friends. It was epic! I felt all grown up.

Being a Teenager

Being a teenager in the 1950s was completely different than it is today. For one thing, we did not have the money to go off drinking and clubbing as they do. We still had our friends from our school days. My friend Marlene Brake was one of them. Most of us were either at the youth club or each other's houses playing LP'S on a gramophone or record player. All the latest hits. Or watching a black and white television. Top of the Pops was a favourite back then. We had lots to talk about, fashion, the latest hairstyles, make up, and not to mention... boys. We often had sleepovers. Our parents did not mind if they had the room.

The cinema, or "The Pictures" as we called it, (I'd often hear others refer to them as "The Flicks") were places most frequented. The Regal in Ashley Road Parkstone was very popular. "I am so sorry it's gone".

The Youth Club

I usually went most Saturday evenings to "The Youth Club". It was at the end of Trinidad Crescent leading into Rossmore Road. There was a Dance. The Jive was all the rage then. You would meet old and make new friends there. A very harmless and fun evening for everyone. Only 5 minutes walk up the road to home at night with our friends. I was told to be home by 10 O'clock and always was. You did as your parents said in those days. It was called "Respect".

The Youth Club – Still standing today!

The Big Bands

Dancing was something we all enjoyed doing. It was a big occasion for us. Then came Ballroom Dancing. As I was not very good at it, my friend Marlene and I decided to have a few lessons. We went to a dancing class in Lower Parkstone. That was such a great laugh. It was the Waltz or Quick-Step. You know one, two, three, turn. If you were energetic enough the Tango. I still cannot dance properly. But it was great fun.

The dances were held in Big Halls. Like the Centenary Hall in Poole. But we used to go to one at Fleetsbridge, which was an Army Drill Hall. There was always a Big Band. Joe Loss Orchestra was a favourite. His band is still going today, but with new musicians of course. These dances were a "Gentleman's Excuse Me" dance. The preparation leading up to it was very exciting. You had to look good, otherwise, you remained a wallflower all evening.

Rock n Roll

The era of Dreamboats and Petticoats. With the Teddy boys in their long coats of many colours. Usually worn with black drainpipe trousers and a flashy waistcoat. A crisp clean, white shirt was always worn with a bootlace tie. They also wore soft shoes, with thick crepe soles and white socks to complement their outfit. Their hair was greased to perfection, with Brylcreem to finalise. They were known as "The Brylcreem Boys". How smart they looked!

The girls also. With their high bouffant hairstyles. That must have taken them an age to prepare, what with all the backcombing and hairspray. The dresses were worn with many a frilled petticoat underneath. A little short-sleeved top and a handkerchief scarf, completing the picture with Ballerina shoes, ankle socks and her make-up.

Friends

I still had my friends from my school days, and Valerie Sargeant was one of those. An only child but not spoilt. We use to go dancing once a month together on a Saturday evening. Her mother did help with clothes for this and Valerie always looked very nice.

After I finished work on that Saturday. I would take my clothes to Valerie's home. They had a bungalow in Mannings Heath Road. Her mother would style my hair for me and Valerie did my make-up. Valerie worked at the cosmetic factory Max Factor, she became an expert at make-up applications. Valerie would have been an excellent ambassador for Max Factor, due to the amount of make-up she wore and owned.

We never stopped dancing! Oh my, how our feet hurt at the end of a great evening. Probably from wearing small heeled shoes with pointed toes. It was a good thing her father picked us up and took us back to Valerie's house. I spent the night at Valerie's as could not go home with all that makeup on.

I was only sixteen after all! my father would have killed me! Wearing lipstick at my age! Forbidden!

The following day her mother cooked us all a gorgeous roast dinner. After all, it was Sunday and most people had a roast on a Sunday. For pudding, we had homemade blackcurrant tart with cream. Yum! Then we played some records on a duke box that you had to wind up. All the latest LP's. How things have changed! Then I would venture home looking like the sweet sixteen I was.

As the saying goes "Old Friends are Gold" and "New Friends are Silver".

And here's another. "Some you forget. Some you would rather forget. Or some you will Never Forget".

And that is mine.

The Tallyman

During the 1950s. The Tallyman was a frequent visitor to homes on "the Estates". He used to call at our house on an early Saturday evening when everyone was at home. He was a kind of salesman.

We welcomed him into our kitchen. He would throw open his large suitcase displaying all of the goodies it contained. Something for all members of a family. He also carried a notebook and pen plus a bundle of payment cards. If you saw something that you liked, you would place an order with him and then he would come back the following week with the item(s). He would give you one of the payment cards with your name on it and write it down in his notebook. Whatever you bought was a shilling a week. He always tried to bring you what you asked for, not to disappoint anyone.

Families did not go out shopping on a Saturday like they do today. They did not earn huge wages. So it served a purpose. They always added a "little" interest. I should think this was the start of the "catalogue business".

The Corner Shops

There was a lot of shops around the roads in Parkstone at one time. It seemed like we had one on every corner.

The first one that I was aware of in Parkstone, was opposite the large wide steps on the right, at the top of the hill in Albert Road. A shortcut we'd often use to Heatherlands School.

"These steps are still there". But the old school has been demolished and new houses built on this site in Cromwell Road.

When the bell rang for the end of the school day. The children tore down those steps to go to the corner shop across the other side of Albert Road. There was very little traffic in those days.

The steps leading to the "Corner Shop"

They sold yellow sherbet to the children for an old penny in this little shop. The sherbet made your tongue and finger yellow when sucked. Or you could buy white sherbet for tuppence. This was mixed with flaked coconut in a paper cone, which I preferred. The old fashion sweets and lollipops were lovely.

On the corner of Dunford Road where it meets Albert Road, on the left side was at one time a Bakery Shop. They always had a window full of nice cakes to tempt you when passing. The baking bread smelt lovely. You could take a loaf home with you straight from their ovens. There is now a plaque above the middle window, which was once the shop door. This reads "Avenue House 1895". Nice to see they've kept the heritage.

At the other end of Dunford Road, where it meets Jubilee Road, on the corner is a white painted house. This was once an Off Licence.

The Village of Parkstone

This little group of corner shops had a village atmosphere.

Everyone seemed to know each other. A very sociable scene. People would not just pass you by, be it in the street or on the little Rossmore Bus. They would talk to each other. Find out what was happening in each other's families. Checking that all was fine and everyone at home was keeping well. People were interested in what was going on around them and if they could help in any way. There was caring for one another.

I remember my father (who was a keen gardener and grew most of our food, very organic) saying to me "take these to a Mrs Meredith". Mrs Meredith had a large family of nine and lived in our road. No money was ever exchanged. It was either some Runner Beans (we always had plenty to spare) or a nice Cabbage and sometimes a bunch of Rhubarb.

In the centre of our front garden, growing in the long border are the most beautiful large Carnations. All colours. And the perfume, WOW! You could smell them when passing by the house. There is nothing like it today, and this I know all too well, as I am an avid gardener myself, even at my age.

One day my father cut a bunch of his favourite Carnations and asked me to please take them to a lady that lived at the far end of the road. My father did this because he had heard from her husband that she was not well. You see this is what the Parkstone people were like.

The Little Chemist

Was on the corner of Albert Road and Rossmore Road at the top of the large hill. It was a lovely small shop which had a pharmacy. So you could collect your prescriptions when needed, without having to travel to Ashley Road. They also sold lots of "over the counter" medications, along with toiletries and failing not to mention, my favourite French perfume. Max Factors make-up was very popular then, also Outdoor Girl was another brand and of course Ponds Cold Cream. Lipsticks were 15d in 1955, all pretty colours. This chemist opposite Hatchards field has been restored and is now a little corner house.

These places were so useful for the Parkstone people. The older inhabitants must miss it.

Gittermans

Gittermans was opposite the chemist and on the corner before the big hill to Ashley Road. When I was eleven years old, many a time, I went whizzing down this hill on my little bike. Fearless back then! It was a small well-stocked shop. Also, the first shop to open on a Sunday. Which did not go down very well with the other shop keepers in the area.

But others soon followed suit. It's called "competition". Quite the opposite nowadays, as there are very few shops in Parkstone that do not open on a Sunday.

The Post Office

A little further along Rossmore Road towards Buckingham Road almost opposite, was the Post Office come general store. This was owned by a Welsh couple.

As well as servicing as a Post Office, they were known as a small grocery store. They had a large help yourself stall outside the shop, selling fruit and veg. But God help those that got caught helping themselves! There was always a friendly greeting when you entered the shop. The Post Office side of the shop was very convenient, as this now would save you a trip up to Ashely Road Post Office.

It has now been turned back into a house, aptly named The Post Office.

The Hairdressers

Was split into two sections, one side for men and the other for women. I used to visit the ladies side of the hairdresser for a special occasion. I would have a "wash and set" or sometimes also a cut. I could not afford to go every week. It was called "rollering" then not blow-drying. The hairdresser would wash my hair facing downward, often spoiling your make-up if wearing. She would finish by putting a hair net over the rollers to keep them in place. Then off to the hooded drier. I used to think it looked like a space helmet. Here you would sit whilst your hair dried reading a magazine. Got very hot sometimes. Once dried, she would brush it through and style as you'd like before finishing with hairspray to keep it all in place. This service cost me 5 shillings.

The Fish n Chip Shop

In 1948-1955, situated at the end of Churchill Road, on the left side, where it meets with Rossmore Road, was a Fish & Chip Shop. I used to be sent there to fetch chips for our family dinner. It was a lovely place. Opening times were at lunch and early evenings until late. There was always a queue even outside the door. While waiting to be served the smell was gorgeous, especially if like me you were hungry.

The chips were cooked from dirt-laden potatoes, dug fresh from the garden. They were washed, peeled, and put through the chippy. You could watch the preparation while you waited. But they were very quick at it. Then they were fried in dripping until light golden in colour and crispy. The flavour was lovely just how I like them. Not like today's chip shop chips, straight from the freezer.

They sold other things, fish of course in batter or breadcrumbed and mushy peas. Which I still love today.

Then came my time to be served. "A shilling's worth of chips please" I would say, with my nose reaching the top of the counter. The assistant placed the chips first on a sheet of white plain paper. Then double wrapped them (ensuring they would arrive home hot) in clean, old "out of date" newspaper obtained from the News Agent across the road. The chips were enough to feed us younger children.

My mother had already prepared something to go with them. Served with Sarsons Vinegar and a sprinkling of salt.

The fish shop did a roaring trade when the Rossmore Pub people turned out at lunch and nighttime closing. A little something for their wives who would be waiting at home for them to come home, whilst the children were fast asleep in bed. The fish and chip shop is still there today. New owners of course. I recently had some fresh Cod and chips from there one lunchtime, not too bad. Then nothing tastes the same as it used to. But the memories of that shop, each time I pass by, are irreplaceable to me.

The Family Butcher

Next to the Fish and "Chippy", right on the corner, opposite the Rossmore Public House was a little Butchers shop. It used to have fresh meat in the window daily.

The butcher would cut with a "chopper" on a wooden chopping block, just what the customer needed.

No prepacked meat in his shop.

The sausages were made from his very own recipe, then hung them up on big metal hooks in his window. You could have just the amount you wanted. No food was ever wasted, if there were any leftovers, these were made into recipes like "Bubble & Squeak". Faggots were another product he sold. They were absolutely lovely. Freshly made by him. My mother used to cook them and serve with potatoes she had dug from our garden, along with freshly picked garden peas, which my father had grown. This was a very hot meal for all the family. It was after the 1939-1945 war and rationing. So people appreciated what food was offered and made the most out of what they could afford.

A joint of meat was bought for a "Sunday roast" only. A half leg of lamb or a shoulder. This cost about 10 shillings in the 1950s. Sometimes we had one of our own reared chickens.

I can see Mother now, sat in the kitchen, a galvanised small bath at her feet, plucking the chicken. She would be covered in feathers. The whole family then sat down to Sunday lunch. Very traditional dinner and time-honoured occasion.

Monday was always homemade cottage pie or shepherd's pie, made from fresh butcher's mince. Or on occasion, we would have bubble and squeak, if there were any leftover potatoes and vegetables from the Sunday roast.

This little butchers shop is still in Parkstone. But is now a sewing business. Still, very useful though.

One of the First

Next to the butchers was a lovely greengrocers shop. They later moved to Ashley Road. Close by was a CO-OP store which I believe was one of the first Co-Op's to introduce "self-service". Meaning, baskets were at the ready and you could help yourself to goods off the shelves on your own - unassisted, then go to the till and pay. Of course, this is how we all shop today!

There was a Drapery store, very 1950s. Also a wool and baby shop next to it. Both shops were frequently used as knitting was very popular then.

Simmons, was on the corner of Good Road and was for many years a really nice old shop. Mr & Mrs Simmons owned it. They too changed over to a "self-service" store. Simmons today is now Co-Op Express shop.

Last Two Standing

Those corner shops, all 37 of them, were part of the character of Parkstone for Parkstone people. "I supported them all" in their time here. So convenient and an absolute joy to visit. Always sold top quality goods. But one by one we lost them to the Ashley Road shops.

Last Man Standing

On a walk recently, I noticed scaffolding surrounding a building in Norrish Road. A building company is in the process of developing flats above the shop. Located on the ground floor is a hairdresser named "Peter John".

Peter did his training at a salon in London. He is a true gentleman and a top-quality hairdresser. He has been doing the hair for the Parkstone people, plus others from neighbouring towns, both males and females, for about thirty-three years at this little salon.

"He cares". Always gives good advice on what he would recommend for your hair. But leaves the decisions entirely a choice for you. Not pushy. He is a top London stylist without the London price tags. He is a good hairdresser, not a miracle worker.

But I can honestly say that I have never seen anyone leaving his salon without looking 100% improved. We need this little shop, it is so convenient and Peter would be greatly missed.

The Little Gospel Hall

It was at the end of Pembrook Road where it joins Rossmore Road. Children were invited to watch silent films here shown on a large white screen. Usually held on Sunday's, early evenings, for about an hour and a half.

Some of the films were Charlie Chaplin (black and white) or "slapstick" comedies with subtitles. The characters appeared to be moving in fast forward mode, which made us all laugh. It was always a fun night. At the end of the film(s), there was a collection box which cost us about tuppence each.

It is still there on the corner.

If we saw an Ariel on a chimney pot or on a roof of a house on our way home. We would say to each other "look up there, they have an Ariel, they must be rich". Very few people owned a television in their home in 1951 in Parkstone. These were usually rented, with black and white pictures. Programmes didn't start until 6 pm and this was usually beginning with The News before regular programmes started.

After dinner, the whole family would sit down to watch the television altogether. The children had to be very quiet. It was a novelty then.

Four Weddings

My parents had four of their daughters get married in the 1950s. All within a few years of each other and at quite a young age.

I was married in St Clement's Church, Newtown. But things were very different then. A young woman thought it was her goal in life to get married. It is not so today. There are lots of opportunities for women today and "marriage" for some, is not the first thing on their minds. A career is!

I think my mother was suffering from the "empty nest syndrome". But she need not have worried. In the 1960s the grandchildren came flooding in and that house, "our house" was never empty again.

My Conclusion

Is Yes!

Parkstone has changed and in some areas not for the better.

But as a child, growing up here in Parkstone and being a poor family from Poole. I can honestly say I did not know what "unhappiness" was. As we always had the support of our good friends and Parkstone neighbours.

Parkstone is changing, but so are the times. What do the Parkstone people have today?

I would conclude this is very much the census in most communities today. But do not let us "Parkstone people" be too negative here. Because if we open our eyes and take a good look around, there are many good restorations and improvements taking place, at this very moment.

Someone once asked me what I missed about Parkstone today? And I replied, "The familiar faces of people I once knew". And of course, I miss the Regal Cinema. However, this is not necessarily a sad matter.

I am just learning to embrace all that is and has become today.

I have travelled much in my lifetime. We live on a beautiful island and Scotland keeps calling me back. I have been to many lovely places in Europe. Italy and France to name but a few. Truly unforgettable experiences. I have ventured to The Caribbean, but believe me "it is not all paradise" even there! When younger I also visited Israel! Literally — I could have kissed the ground of English soil when I returned. But if there is one thing that I have learnt from it all, is I will always be;

A Parkstone Girl.

Printed in Great Britain
by Amazon

72716351R00048